The Island

The Island

A young boy's journey to manhood on Matinicus Island

Stephen Cronin's account of his transformation from a troubled youth to a productive young adult through the power of love and guidance.

Stephen Cronin
As told to Marian Wells Cronin

iUniverse, Inc.

New York Lincoln Shanghai

The Island
A young boy's journey to manhood on Matinicus Island

iUniverse books may be ordered through booksellers or by contacting:

iUniverse
2021 Pine Lake Road, Suite 100
Lincoln, NE 68512
www.iuniverse.com
1-800-Authors (1-800-288-4677)

The views expressed in this work are solely those of the author and do not necessarily reflect the views of the publisher, and the publisher hereby disclaims any responsibility for them.

ISBN-13: 978-0-595-39149-3 (pbk)
ISBN-13: 978-0-595-83535-5 (ebk)
ISBN-10: 0-595-39149-4 (pbk)
ISBN-10: 0-595-83535-X (ebk)

Printed in the United States of America

In honor of the pluck and resiliency of our nation's children.

North

Two Bush
Island

Field Point

High Point

West Point

Young Point

MATINICUS ISLAND

Matinicus
Harbor

Little Island

Wheaton
Island

Black Rocks

Condon
Point

Curtis Point

Southwest
Point

Cato
Cove

Tenpound
Island

Contents

A Note to the Reader

Matinicus Island sits quietly 22 miles off the coast of southern Maine, at the entrance to Penobscot Bay. A scant two miles long and a mile wide, it rises no more than 100 feet above the ocean at its highest point.

Throughout the island's history humans have fished, farmed and grazed, drawing on the natural resources which abound on and around this rise of land in the Atlantic. Until the mid 1700's Penobscot Indians hunted seals and gathered bird eggs on the island's shores. By the early 1800's white settlers occupied almost all available land, establishing permanent farms and constructing shacks for drying fish or building boats.

The events in this autobiography take place in the mid 1800's, just as the island population peaked at 277 hardy individuals. Residents fished for cod, mackerel or herring; raised vegetables or planted grains for their cattle. Life was difficult. The isolation from the mainland compounded the rigors of the fierce Maine winters, the dangers of fishing in the North Atlantic and the challenges of farming in rocky soil hampered by short growing seasons.

Stephen Cronin, at the age of 11, was sent by his widowed mother to live with Freeman Hall and his wife to earn his keep on their Matinicus Island farm. Stephen's account of his life, friendships and growing pains provides an authentic window into the challenges and the bare-bones simplicity of life on Matinicus in the mid 1800's.

Seventy years after leaving Matinicus Island Stephen Cronin recounted these childhood memories to his niece, Marian Cronin. This family treasure is now reprinted for others to enjoy.

Stephen Cronin's life on Matinicus Island illuminates the rural and maritime culture of residents in southeast Maine during the mid 1800's. Readers who wish to learn more about the history or residents of Matinicus Island are encouraged to dig into the references in the back of this book. The Matinicus Island Chamber of Commerce, with its helpful volunteer staff, is also a rich source of island information.

David Jones
Edmonds, WA 2007

Thank you to the following for their contribution to this publication:

Harriet and Warren Williams of the Matinicus Chamber of Commerce for providing maps and historical background of Matinicus Island, John for preserving our family documents, Karen for her careful editing and proofreading of the text, and Cynthia for her patience and encouragement throughout.

And, my profound thank you to *Grandfather* and *Grandmother* Hall for their guidance and love of my Great Grandfather, Stephen Cronin.

Preface

I'm telling these yarns about my childhood in this early spring of my eighty-eighth year, and my memory is kind of hazy concerning dates and distances but it is powerful clear and plain regarding the debt I owe the three folks who had the steering of my boyhood. If I've erred in some of the names of places and people, I pray to be forgiven, as I can't rightly keep all the events straight.

In one thing I'll not err, you can be dead certain. That's in telling of the goodness and kindness of Ellen and Grandfather and Grandmother Hall. I hope and pray my children and grandchildren will never forget those three and will try to pass on to others, as I've tried to, the sacrificing care and love Ellen gave me and the patient guidance and generosity the Halls bestowed on a homeless Irish lad.

Ellen was a hardworking and God-fearing woman who put the welfare of her two fatherless lads above everything else, even to giving them up, and though she knew sorrows and hardships aplenty, she never wavered from doing her best for us.

Grandfather and Grandmother Hall walked in the ways of God and lived up to the principles and teachings of Christ as near as any souls I've ever known and I hope my children will reverence the name of Hall all of their days.

There are two others who are vivid and clear in my mind and they are Will and Alex, my island chums and mates on many a prank and childish ventures.

I'd like to pay my respects to all those souls on Matinicus who made my life as happy a one as any boy ever has known.

Stephen Cronin, 1938

Chapter 1
Caged Up

———————◆———————

My earliest memories are of being shut in one bare room and longing to be out free and roving in the air and sunshine. It wasn't Ellen's fault that we, that is, brother John and I, were shut up so. There was just nothing else she could have done to keep us safe, while she was off washing clothes and scrubbing floors in other folk's houses. It hadn't always been that way. When we were little and while father was alive she'd cared for us and watched over us day and night. But when his vessel and all hands were lost at sea and no word was ever heard of either boat or crew, she had to become the provider.

My father and mother were both Irish immigrants, who'd only been in this country six months when I was born. They'd settled in Rockland while I was a little tad and it was there John was born.

With no man to provide for her and her babies, and not being able to read or write, there was only one way for Ellen to earn and that was to hire out by the day as a scrubwoman.

That's how it happened we were locked up so. In those days folks looked down on the Irish as being ignorant immigrants,

only fit to do the dirty, heavy work about town. Insults and belit-
tling names were hurled at them and often a few stones to boot.
But the Irish were a good-natured people, on the whole, and
they fought back and laughed off the insults and made themselves part of the country.

As I started out to tell in the beginning of this yarn, my first
recollections are of being like a little wild thing, caged up.

When Ellen went off to work in the morning, she put everything we could hurt ourselves with in the other room of our two
rooms. She'd leave a bucket of water, a bit of cold potatoes and
bread on the table and strings and such things as she could provide for toys on the floor. We'd spend the day playing and fighting and sleeping. In winter the room grew cold toward night
as she'd not dare leave us near a stove or fire. Summer was the
worst. The room got hot and stuffy and the days seemed never-
ending with all outdoors calling.

Evenings were nice. When Ellen got home from work we'd
run around and around our two rooms, like young colts let into
pasture. Sometimes she'd have some piece of cake or pie, slipped
out from her own dinner if it happened her lady that day was a
generous one. Some fed the help mighty scanty but others set a
bountiful table, even for those they hired.

After supper we'd romp and play until we were tired and then
Ellen would take us in her lap and tell us tales of her own girl-
hood in Ireland, and in the telling ease her homesickness.

The day always ended with us kneeling beside her, in front of
the crucifix and listening while she said prayers to the Blessed
Virgin.

Sundays were nicest of all. Ellen dressed us in our best and we went to mass and sat proud and happy in our own pew. Times were never so hard that Ellen didn't keep up her pew rent.

Sunday afternoons John and I were turned loose to play outside and it was those afternoons which set such a longing up in me, on week days. The older I got the worse I hated being shut up. I remember in particular the day I broke my jail.

It was unseasonably hot even for a Maine summer day. In the morning while fighting, John and I upset the water bucket and so thirst was added to our misery. John finally cried himself to sleep but I prowled around and around the room like some cub bear in a pen. Between prowls I peered out the window, and finally in a sort of frenzy I started pounding on it with my fists, like a crazy thing.

The window rattled loose in the casing and all at once an idea came to me. I'd escape if I had to break out. I tugged and pushed and finally, by standing on a small keg, I got that window up enough to crawl through. We lived on the ground floor of the tenement so it was no great drop to the ground. I let the keg down first, to use against our return, and then lowered John out and followed.

We were scared and timid as we slipped down the alley. Fear of being seen kept us behind a shed the rest of the afternoon, but the sun and fresh cool air blowing on our hot bodies was treat enough.

Before dark we got ourselves back in and the window closed so Ellen did not suspect anything.

Each day we ventured further afield and even down along the wharfs to see the fishing boats and big masted schooners lying at anchor. Our curiosity at the strange sights made us tarry longer each day, and finally we overstayed our time. When we got home, considerably after dark, Ellen and the neighbors were all hunting for us. The open window and the keg underneath had told the story plain enough.

Ellen, in relief from being frightened most to death, hugged us and then she whipped us hard and we promised to stay at home.

I wish I could say we were good boys and minded, but such was not the case. Next day, all at once that same shut-in, frantic feeling hit me. It was worse, for having tasted escape! At last I got us out, calculating that air and sunshine and space were worth a hard whipping every night.

Sometimes we were caught and punished but oftener we fooled Ellen and beat her home.

From those days on, I've always had a hunger for space and freedom and hated being cramped and held down too close.

Chapter 2

The Big House

Ellen scolded and whipped us for running away, until she saw she was wasting her efforts and then she talked over the problem with some of her ladies, who had really taken a kindly interest in us.

These ladies in turn spoke to husbands and the upshot of it was, a house was found for us, with room enough for a dozen boys to romp around.

A law suit was going on over a big dwelling house that had stood vacant for a mighty long time. The house was owned by Cobb, White and Case, the general merchandising company. They had a whole passel of ships and kept store to outfit them.

It seems possession was nine points to law and the company figured Ellen might as well be in possession rent free as any other soul, thereby benefiting all parties.

The house really was a big one, with more rooms than I can count by memory, and an ell and wood shed and a sort of court yard. Just to prove how big it was, it was later turned around and made into two sizable store buildings.

Ellen had scarcely enough furniture for two rooms, so the rest belonged to John and me, to make ourselves at home in. We were wide awake and right on deck to take advantage of this and before long had the place filled with playmates. All day we were free to run and plan without let or hindrance, and a mighty happy time was had by all of us. We didn't need toys for entertainment. Space, boys and imagination provided that. Indian and soldier and pirates were our favorite games.

We were mighty comfortable and happy though Ellen was able to make only a chancy living. Sometimes her ladies put off paying and then we were hard put for food of any kind, other times the ladies were generous with work and treats from their tables and we felt like kings, eating warmed-over meat and pie.

An event occurred which made us appreciate all our benefits as we had not before. One noon, just as we started dinner, a big lummox of a man clumped in and without a by-your-leave or anything started throwing the furniture into the yard. We found later it was old man Halley, agent for the parties who were trying to get the house.

Ellen sent me on the run for help from Cobb, White and Case. I was crying hard as I could and about winded when I reached the store. First of all, it seemed entirely empty, it being noon and all hands out for dinner. Finally, in the back I located Alden Litchfield and gasped, between sobs, "A man is over at the house throwing Mother's things out and she says to come quick!"

Alden didn't wait to even grab a hat, but went on the run, me following on his heels. When we reached the dooryard Alden shouted, "Halley, get out before I kick you out!"

Old Halley grumbled and muttered but Alden stood over him until he beat a retreat. Then Alden helped carry the table and chairs back in and said he guessed it could be fixed so that we would not be bothered again.

When the excitement was over, Ellen cried and cried, and John and I joined in to keep her company, until all at once Ellen dried her eyes and said, "Stephen, did you chop the wood this morning?"

I said I'd had to go to the wharf with Mike O'Toole on an errand but I'd do the wood in the afternoon. She said, "I'll fix you so you won't go loafing off with the O'Tooles whilst there's wood to be cut. I guess likely you're big enough to take a share in the work hereabouts and I'll fix you so you'll stay alongside that wood until it's cut. If I can't whip you into staying home, I'll shame you into keeping out of sight of that whole raft of young hoodlums you're always chasing off with."

Thereupon she made me take off every stitch of clothes and locked them in the cupboard. Then she tied an old white petticoat under my arms, saying, "I guess you'll not want the boys to be seeing you in that garb. Now get to the woodshed and stay there!"

At first I was mad, clear through, but as I pondered my situation I got that shut-in desperate feeling and twixt anger and despair I was in a state. At first, with every axe blow, the petticoat got in the way and I'd cut it. This made quite an interesting game and I finally cooled down, intent on seeing how riddled I could make that petticoat by night, endeavoring to make a rent with every blow.

When Mother came home, I was a sight, being dressed in strings, almost, but she didn't say a word. She just handed me my clothes with orders to wash up in a hurry. Her mouth kept twitching and I knew she was having a hard time not to laugh.

She'd brought a bit of cooked meat and some cornbread, so we feasted like lords. It was warm and snug and safe inside, after all the excitement and perils of the day. John and I knelt down, quiet and good, before the Virgin while Ellen said prayers for us all including our lost father.

Chapter 3
Pigs and Taunts

———————————◼———————————

Times were hard and Ellen was put to it to feed and clothe us, let alone lay by enough for the winter's fuel. There was scarcely a week she got work every day and the pay was nothing to brag about. She'd been a mighty comely Irish lass, but already she was looking warn and driven. Her hands were cracked from lye in the wash water and her knees sore from kneeling to scrub. As I look back, I marvel that she kept so patient and cheerful.

John and I took little thought for the coming winter, but Ellen was so worried she finally talked to her ladies and worked out a plan which would keep me busy and out of mischief and help with the fuel supply.

I was all for anything new and fell right in with the idea. Mother brought two little pigs, which John and I made over and thought powerful cute. We fixed a pen in the shed and then I started out collecting garbage, which Ellen's ladies had promised to save.

My first day out was a nightmare. The slop smelled terrible to begin with, and the buckets were heavy. To make it worse, as I neared home, on the last trip, a big lout reached out a foot and tripped me, so I fell and was covered with the mess. A gang of boys gathered about, as my cries filled the air and they all started yelling, "Look at Sloppy! Look at Sloppy!"

They fell in behind me and followed me all the way home with taunts and catcalls.

That night I cried and cried, declaring I'd carry no more swill.

Ellen cleaned me up and then took me on her lap to explain all over again. "Now Stephen darling. Do be a good boy and help you mother. Look, if you'll just feed the pigs this summer, I'll be buying some corn in the fall and fatten them proper. Then we'll sell one and keep one. Just think how nice some fat meat will be tasting next winter and how fine you and John will look in new suits from the sale of the other pig. Don't pay any heed to the hoodlums when they torment you and don't fight unless you have to."

With each day of the passing summer a new name was added to the list. I was known as "Piggy", "Irish Piggy", "Smelly Stephen", and "Sloppy." Even the grown loafers held their noses when I passed.

After being tripped more times than one I learned to fight, but being little and skinny I got the worst of it, usually. For every pound that went on those pigs I got a black eye or bruise and shed many a bitter tear.

Seems that was the year I learned to use my fists and yell back foul words equal to any I received.

If it hadn't been for Ellen, I'd have given up. She praised me and scolded me and held me to the job.

When fall came the pigs were fattened on corn, as she'd promised and then all but a fourth of one was sold.

One evening when John and I got home, late as usual, from our rambles Ellen, all smiles, was waiting in the doorway. She was acting mighty mysterious as she let us in. There spread out was worsted for new suits for each of us, as a reward for the summer's torment.

The death of the pigs didn't end my troubles. All any boy had to do to make me fighting mad was to hold his nose and yell, "Swill Bucket!" It took many a blow before I lived down the summer's business.

Chapter 4
A Disappointment

With the coming of fall I fell from the frying pan into the fire, seems as though. Encouraged by her ladies, Ellen mulled over the idea of educating me as she and my father had planned; the first step being to enter me in public school, though in the back of her own mind the ambition was growing to make a priest of me.

She'd rather have sent me to parochial school, but we were too poor to pay the entrance fee. She tried to balance that by dragging me to mass and entering me in the catechism class.

I didn't mind mass so much, though I got terribly fidgety and squirmed about until Ellen would pinch my ear to settle me down.

I never could remember, on purpose, to take my catechism to class; being as I'd never studied it. The priest would say on such occasions, "Stephen, if you don't bring your catechism next time I'll be canning you proper."

I learned by experience that if I skipped the next class he would forget all about his threat. That's how come I missed more often than I attended. What with playing hooky from catechism and being inattentive at mass, my chances of becoming a priest were slim.

School was worst of all. I could stand just a few days and then I'd be away to the wharfs. I'd lay at my moorings about so long, then that shut-in, cramped feeling would get the better of me and off I'd go, on a fine, frosty, fall morning.

Falls are a lovely time in Maine, with the birches and sassafras all in color.

The wharfs drew me like a magnet. Boats of all kinds lay at anchor, crewed by sailors from every nation on the face of the globe; mostly English and Spanish and French and Dutch. Some sailors had big mustaches and rings in their ears like pirates.

The air was filled with the smell of fruits and tar and spices and hemp. There were boats from the West Indies and other far places, bringing in tea and rice and hemp and taking off with lime and lumber.

Some of the boats had figures of women or eagles on their prows. These were painted in gay colors which dazzled my eyes.

My ears were filled with the sound of the crack and rattle of the ships at work. There was laughter and shouting in strange tongues; and such swearing as only seafaring men can blue the air with.

It's no wonder a boy would ship his moorings and make for the wharfs on such days. Geography out of a book was tame compared to geography learned by viewing ships and men from many of the world's ports.

While I played hooky by day Ellen worked nights sewing our new suits. She was happier and did more laughing than at any time since she'd been widowed. I guess just the security of a few dollars ahead gave her relief from her anxiety.

At last, on a fine Sunday morning we were all decked out in our best bib and tucker. The money from the pigs had stretched out farther than you'd believe.

John and I had new suits and boots. Ellen was fixed up in a new shawl and fresh ribbons on her bonnet, and she carried herself mighty proud as she went up the aisle to mass.

The service was extra long. My new worsted itched me and my feet seemed on fire, as the new boots were stiff and hot after having run barefoot all summer.

During the sermon there was a commotion in the O'Toole's pew, behind us. So, I climbed on my knees and turned around to take it in. Ellen, dozing along comfortably, came to with a start, and before you could say Jack Robinson, she gave my ear a cuff that most upended me.

"Stephen! Sit down!" she hissed, so loud the O'Toole boys heard. They started snickering and I knew they were enjoying my shame.

The rest of the service I sulked, feeling sorry for myself and working up a good mad at Ellen.

As we left the church all the whistles in town began to blow.

"Fire!" someone yelled. I had no more use for Mother, but was off like a shot.

"It's the lime kilns!" a man called.

The sound increased as we rushed up the street, and I was carried along in the thick of it.

At the kilns, I wiggled my way up to the front of the line, and all agog with excitement, took my stand by the fire truck.

Mr. Libby spied me and led me to where the men were working the pumps for dear life. He hoisted me on a pile of ashes so that I could grab a handle, and I pumped away as big as the next fellow.

I sure had me a wonderful time. Women from town brought food and coffee, and I sat right up with the men and ate my share, feeling like a hero.

By evening the fire was out, and folks and engines scattered, and I had time to take stock of myself.

I was such a mess as you never saw in your life. Lime dust, soot, smoke and water had done their worst. My suit was torn out at the sleeves and ruined, the new boots, all scuffed and whitened, looked a year old.

For the first time that afternoon, I thought of Ellen and the whipping that would be waiting for me, and I walked slower and slower.

Home at last, I went in the back way, hoping to sneak to bed unnoticed. Ellen was laying in wait for me, though, and called me to the kitchen.

One look at me was enough. "Oh, Stephen! How could you do such a thing? Your new suit and boots are all ruined! Mercy knows—there will never be money for more!" and throwing up her apron over her head she rocked back and forth, sobbing as though her heart would break.

Not another word did she say, and I crept off to bed, made more miserable by her sobs than I'd have been from a dozen beatings.

Chapter 5

Ellen's Decision

The city's streets are a wonderful education for a lad. They put him on his own resources, to sink or swim. If he's lucky enough to be led in the right direction it will be the making of him. It's more often the case he's led wrongly, and the streets are his undoing.

The wharfs and alleyways taught me to use my wits, and my fists—and according to my luck with both of them, I had good days and bad ones.

As time went on, I roamed farther afield from home and school, listening to yarns told by sailors in lofts and warehouses. Those men were as full of yarns as a knitting bag, and I never tired of hearing of the ports they'd been to and the vessels they'd sailed.

Outside of Rockland lay the stone quarries which provided the town with the material for its principle business, which was the making of lime.

Whole forests of wood were used to fire the ovens of the lime kilns, and the wood smoke hung heavy and sharp in the air from one day to the next. Fish and salt water and wood smoke were all combined to be the smell of Rockland.

I was getting older and stronger now, and big enough to earn a dollar here and there to help out at home. Preferring work to school, we boys hung about the kilns on the chance of picking up a day's job.

The lime was drawn from the kiln twice every twenty-four hours and then packed in barrels ready for loading. Now, loading was done in the following manner: the barrels were picked up by clamps, which were fastened to block and tackle on a boom. These were swung out and dropped into the holds of the vessels.

Our job was to fasten the clamp on the barrels and, though it wasn't heavy work, we rightly earned the fifty cents a day we were paid.

The Civil War brought me a new way of earning, which was by selling a newspaper called "The War Cry." Excitement ran high about the town and my new job satisfied me completely, it giving me an excuse to hang about the streets and wharfs. I rambled through sail lofts and onto boats, wherever I'd see a knot of men.

I got madder than a hornet when one man would buy a paper and all hands fall in to read over his shoulder, instead of buying their own.

Rockland was full of big mercantile shops, furnishing supplies for the ships. Up over these stores there were great lofts used by day for the making of sails and nets, and by night for lodge meetings and such.

The militia used these lofts to drill, so whenever there was drilling, you'd find a gang of boys, taking it all in.

Wasn't long before we knew all the maneuvers as well as the men did, and the ambition of every red-blooded lad was to become a drummer boy and go off to war.

I got filled with all sorts of top lofty notions and finally went to the recruiting office to sign up for service. The officer, acting serious as could be, stood me up against the door jam to get my height. He looked me all over and then said, "You're a might short according to specifications. Come back day after tomorrow and if you've grown enough by then, I'll enlist you."

Well, I went every other day for weeks and was measured, but goodness, I didn't know a boy could grow so slow.

Excitement was white hot when the Forth Main sailed for the front. All the bands were playing and men shouting and women crying, as the soldiers marched onto the Daniel Webster. I recollect it was so heavily loaded it was sunk right down to the guards.

Watching the militia and selling papers kept me busy by day, and the theatres and taverns lured me by night.

Our gang learned to wait until the ticket collectors left the door and then we'd slip in and see the tail end of the show. I don't remember the name of a single show now, but I found them exciting at the time.

After being out so late, I was afraid to go home because I knew Ellen would whip me proper, so I'd make it to the lime kilns. I usually knew the fireman and so could be certain of the loan of an old coat or blanket to sleep on. The ground, even in coldest weather, was warm in front of the ovens, and I loved to sleep there. Sometimes, with no other reason than just to be free of walls, I'd go there to sleep.

I learned to get home early the following day, so Ellen would find me wonderful good and active, chopping wood, and I'd use soft soap and all the blarney in me to turn away her wrath.

Our gang got into so many fights and scrapes that we were in danger of running afoul of the law, and everyone prophesied we'd all land in the reformatory, if we didn't mend our ways.

Ellen was so worried about me, she finally bound me out, to work upstate, on a farm.

I don't care to recall those days, as they were like a bad dream. I wasn't much good at work, I'll admit, but I do believe the whippings I got were pretty severe and those farmers were asking a lot of labor of a skinny boy.

Well, I failed first one place and then another, being sent home with the message I wasn't worth my board and keep. Ellen was about desperate and talked me over with all her ladies.

A sort of Red Cross sewing meeting was being held at the Owl's Head and the women got to discussing Ellen and her problem. One of the ladies said she believed her father might be interested in taking me. She promised to write to Matinicus Island, where he lived, and see what could be done.

Several letters passed back and forth, and interviews were had with Ellen. The upshot was, the Halls at Matinicus agreed to try me out for the summer.

Threat of the reformatory had sobered me down some, so I was eager and willing to be given one last chance.

Ellen got my few clothes ready and when word came there was a packet sailing for Matinicus, we hurried to the pier.

She kept her arm about me and cried as it came time to part and her last words were, "Stephen, I want you to be a good boy and behave yourself. Don't fight. I don't want you sent home in disgrace."

I gave my promise, really meaning to keep it.

I've been asked if I was fearful, going off that way to sea and to strange people.

That, I was not. I'd made my way with rough sailors and land bullies on the streets most of my life and I'd no reason to think I'd fare worse in a new place.

Then too, I was powerful excited over the whole adventure. I'd broke the bars of home and Rockland and now I'd more space to move about in.

Chapter 6
Crossing to a New Life

———————◆———————

Regular packets weren't running in those days, so mail and passengers and freight were carried more or less haphazardly, depending on chance boats and the weather.

The vessel I was sailing on was loaded with freight and carrying a few passengers, beside the crew. It was a sparkling clear day—I can remember it after all of this time. The water on such days was deep blue-green and the sky was the color of a turquoise stone. As we left the harbor I had my last glimpse of Rockland and the green Camden hills running down to meet the ocean. We passed Owl's Head and then before me was the Atlantic, big and boundless.

Matinicus is the largest of the group of islands guarding the entrance to Penobscot Bay, and just one of a quite a number. These islands and ledges make the waters dangerous and that's why there are so many lights and buoys.

It took a smart and brave man to navigate those waters, especially during the war. The British privateers were preying on our vessels and destroying lights all up and down the coast, though they found their mistake, later, when the Canadian boats piled up on the ledges, for lack of lights to steer by.

Not long before I went to the Island the privateer The Tallahassee came across the Matinicus fishing fleet and after driving all the men onto one boat, they burned the rest, just for pure cussedness.

Matinicus—as I was saying—is the most important, being two miles long and a mile wide. I'll be telling you more about it later.

There's Ragged Island, where the Cries lived, then Wooden Ball, so named because it's bare and round, and Two Bush, and Seal Island, and Pudding Island and No Man's Land and Ten Pound. During the Revolution the British preyed on the islands, stealing cattle and killing people. A ten pound cannon ball was found later, giving that island its name.

Most useful to navigation, of all the smaller islands, is Matinicus Rock, where the big lights are. There's a wonderful history behind the brave keepers of those lights.

Why, the summer I went out, Mr. Grant Scott, the keeper, was watching for privateers and sending signals to the fishing fleet when there was any danger.

He had a daughter by the name of Mary, who could handle a boat like a man. She was having a great sport that summer, taking her town friends out in the dories for a ride, and watching for signals. He'd hoist a flag whenever a privateer appeared in the distance and she'd make it for shore in a hurry.

Well, I veered a long way off the course of my story, but I want all hands reading this to get the geography of the place straight.

As I was saying, it was as perfect a sailing day as you'd hope to see, when I made my first journey to Matinicus.

I was all eyes and excitement. The water was so clear and clean, different from what I'd been used to around the wharfs at home. The air, so free from smoke, almost made me drunk it was so pure, and the taste of the salt spray on my lips was a joy.

As we drew near the Island, which looked like a green, tree-covered boat floating in the ocean, we began to see the white sails of the fishing fleet, like birds with white wings.

We drew into the harbor and after saying good-bye to the captain, I stepped foot on the Island wharf, my bundle in one hand and my cap in the other—eleven years old and all ready to meet what came my way, head on, with a full sail.

Chapter 7

A Room of One's Own

If I live to be a hundred, I'll never forget my first glimpse of Grandfather Hall as he stood on the wharf. I guess he wasn't overly tall but there was such a calm and dignified way about him, he seemed head and shoulders above the general run of man—at least that was my way of thinking. He had gray hair and a gray fringe of a beard and the keenest eyes you ever saw. They were piercing and probing but tempered with a twinkle.

He was garbed in working clothes, but so clean and neat he gave the impression of being dressed like a judge.

I thought he looked stern—until he smiled. Then his face was gentle and kind as could be, so that my fear left as he came forward to greet me.

By the hand he led a little girl a mite younger than I was, and when she smiled I grinned back.

"So you're Stephen Cronin," says Grandfather Hall as he took my hand. "We're right pleased you've come. This is my granddaughter Ella, who makes her home with us too, and I presume likely you'll get acquainted before the summer's over."

"You hungry after your voyage? I expect we'd better get on home, it's more than past our dinner hour."

We'd made wonderful good time, as the wind was favorable and the sea just right for a boat to fairly fly.

For once my Irish tongue was checked and all I could do was grin from ear to ear and fall in beside him and Ella. He took my bundle and led the way up a steep and rocky lane to the oxen road, and then the Island was spread before my eyes. It was a pretty picture made up of white houses and green trees and fields and a clear blue sky overhead. There's no handsomer place on earth, to my way of thinking, than the Island. There's just two words to describe it—neat and clean—and by neat I mean all shipshape and trimmed with flower beds in dooryards, and wild ones on hills and pastures, and birds a-flying and the smell of spruce and bayberry in the air. I hope when I get to Heaven it'll be something like the Island and peopled with the same sort of kindly folks.

At last we came to a big plain white house, with green grass and flowers in the yard and the paned fanlight over the front doorway sparkling like jewels. There was myrtle on either side of the door and a big conch shell on the step. The old gentleman led us round to the back through the woodshed and summer kitchen to the kitchen proper.

There, sitting in a sunny window rocking and knitting, was a little old lady, as spick and tidy as the house. She put her knitting up and when she got to her feet I realized she was lame.

"So this is Stephen," she said, as I went forward with my hand out, as Ellen had coached me to do. Instead of shaking as I'd expected, she leaned over and kissed me, as though I was already her own.

"You're welcome here and I hope you'll like us as much as we're going to like you. Now come, come, dinner's late and getting cold. You, Ella, show Stephen where to wash up and come help me set the victuals on."

When I slipped into my place at table I was feeling happy and bashful at the same time. First off, when they all bowed heads for the old gentleman to say grace I didn't know what it was about, but seeing Ella folding her hands and bowing her head, I did likewise.

The voyage and excitement had made me powerful hungry, so I ate with relish of the boiled potatoes and fish and cold soda biscuit spread with jam. I about foundered before the deep custard pie was set on, but I managed to do justice by a slab of it—there's no custard pie on earth to equal the Island kind, made in a deep pan with enough filling to get your teeth into.

After Ella had helped with the dishes she showed me over the place, which seemed big and rambling. The inside was scrubbed clean as a deck and homelike with rag rugs on the floors and curtains at the windows. There were books and papers about and things carved out of wood and things brought by seafaring men from far ports.

The house was built around a big center chimney and fireplace, and made strong and durable for families to grow up and really live in. Upstairs the chambers had sloping ceilings and from every window there was a view of the ocean, and hills and woods.

Amanda Howard, she who was Amanda Hall, and her husband Charles had their apartment in part of the upstairs, and Ella and I had our rooms above, too.

We rambled all over the forty acre farm and I got acquainted with the oxen and the cows, and the inside of the big white barn, which was shared in partnership with the Philbrooks.

Next we went down to the wharves and rambled around and it was quite a different sight than now. There was about thirty vessels leaving harbor at the beginning of the season, to fish for cod and mackerel and herring from Newfoundland to the Bay of Fundy. In the fall when the fleet came in the salted fish were dried in the Island fish houses and taken to the mainland.

There were fish houses and workshops for the repairing and building of craft. Most of the Islanders were farmers, fishermen, and carpenters all rolled into one. The large general store was owned by the Youngs, who sold everything from groceries to seamen's outfits.

Grandfather Hall had held every office on the Island and at the time I went there was Postmaster—for which service he was paid something like fifteen dollars a year. Beside the farm he had an interest in some vessels and owned a smoke house and a salt house along the wharf.

He was a sort of arbitrator for disputes and held to be fair and square in all his dealings, so his word was as good as his bond.

While rambling through the salt house we came upon Grandfather at work. He sent Ella on home and leading me outside, sat down on a keg and indicated for me to fall alongside.

He talked some of the Island and its ways and then got to the matter he had in mind.

"Stephen," says he, "I know you've leaned a lot of bad ways and foul language from hanging about the wharfs on the mainland. We don't hold with that sort of talk in our home, so I'll have to ask you to set a watch on your speech and exercise care in what you say. When you hear me swearing or using profanity—you may—but not until then."

"We're simple folks and haven't much money, but we've food and a roof which you're welcome to, but if you want to be enjoying of those things you'll have to share the producing of them—that's a fair and square proposition, seems though."

"One other thing. Spare Grandmother all you can. Along with the rest of us, you'll have to save her from unnecessary steps."

I'd been glib enough on the streets, but this man-to-man talk was different from any I'd ever experienced and while I was wonderfully impressed, I'd no words to explain my feelings, except to mumble that I'd do my best.

Grandfather closed up the salt house and we went on home where I got my first taste of helping, by carrying in wood and water.

Time supper was over, I was numb with sleepiness, hardly keeping awake until family prayers were said and I could go aloft and turn in.

The little chamber, tucked under the eaves, was the first I'd ever had to myself. I felt like a captain in a yacht cabin. There was a narrow spool bed with a feather mattress and a crazy quilt for a coverlet and a chest and a rocker; and by the bed a strip of rag rug. On the wall hung a colored chrome of a ship in a storm.

I knelt down and said prayers to the Virgin, as I'd promised Ellen I would, and then crept between the clean covers.

Outside, the little waves lapped on the beach and once in a while the soft note of the bell buoy made its music, lulling me to slumber as Ellen's songs had when I was a little child.

Chapter 8

Island Life

Life soon settled into a kind of pattern of work and play, though the playing was mostly done right at home. Seems likely Grandfather thought best to keep me on a short tether until he'd more or less tried me out. Because of this, I didn't get acquainted much outside the family that first summer.

There was a pervading spirit of peace hanging over the whole place; it gentled even a fighting Irish lad. We went along on an even keel all the time, and bad behavior was discouraged in such a nice way—it was easier being good than I'd feared it would be.

Ella and I hadn't many toys to play with, except those we made for ourselves out of material at hand, but there were books about the house and a children's magazine called "The School Mate."

Evenings were the best part of the day, with Grandfather telling yarns and Grandmother sitting in her rocker knitting or spinning and Ella and me on the floor listening.

For the spinning the old lady had an extra large rocker; because of lameness she couldn't walk back and forth from the wheel.

She'd get her distance by rocking clear back and in that way spin as much yarn as any woman on the Island.

Summer brought plowing and planting with work aplenty for all hands. In fact, the whole Island fairly hummed with business. Everyone left on the Island, after the fleet sailed, labored from sunup to sundown. Life wasn't easy and the land was sort of hardscrabble and rocky so it had to be handled carefully. The children worked in the fields, hoeing potatoes and pulling weeds and turning hay, a job which had to be done over and over. Sunny days weren't too plentiful and it was a problem to get the sweet smelling hay dried out. One of my stints was to turn it, when the sun shone and the wind blew the fog away.

Then, there was the never ending task of keeping the wood box filled. It was beyond me how a stove could burn so much fuel as ours did. The part I liked best was when we took the oxen and the cart to the beach to gather driftwood. There was time for me to daydream of all the far ports the pieces had come from and imagine the names of wrecks that they had been part of.

While I tended the wood box and the chores, Ella helped inside, running from kitchen to pantry and up and down the cellar stairs. Grandmother used to say Ella was her flying feet.

Most women, lame as Grandmother, would have given up and taken to the life of an invalid—but not her. Being too lame to stand much, she did her work sitting, or on her knees—as on wash days when she set the tubs on the floor, and kneeling before them, scrubbed and rinsed and wrung, until the garments on our line were clean as any you'd ever see.

Grandfather and Grandmother Hall had raised eight or nine children of their own and several others belonging to relatives. Now, in their old age, they'd taken on Ella and me.

We had the only large farm on the Island, so the rest looked to us for their root vegetables, especially potatoes, which Grandfather traded for fish when the fleet came in.

Everyone, as I said, worked. The men left at home were busy at the wharfs, cleaning, salting and drying the fish that came in on the dories and repairing gear and such.

The women and girls gardened and spun; and wove and sewed; also when need arose worked in the fields. They laid by everything that could be gathered—against the long winter months. Apples were cut and strung to dry; there were wild strawberries and blackberries and huckleberries to make into jams; and cranberries to be gathered for the market. There were chickens to tend and motherless lambs to be raised by hand.

Sundays were the nicest of the days of the week. Different from many of the Islanders who worked all seven days through, Grandfather was a great observer of the Sabbath. Not a turn of labor went on, except the feeding of the animals. The day was given over to rest and meditation, a thing which was mighty beneficial to us all.

There being no church on the Island, there weren't any meetings to attend, except occasionally when the missionary boat came our way. That's how so many happened to spend the Lord's day like any other.

Soon as the Sunday dinner work was done, Grandfather and Grandmother would settle down in the parlor which was only used then and for company. If it was cool they'd have a blaze going in the fireplace. Grandfather would read to Grandmother from the Bible on his knees until she'd fall asleep and then to himself until he'd drop off too, and then they'd doze the time away until evening.

Chapter 9
School Trouble

Late August storms marked the close of summer and the return of the fleet for a time, so the scenes of my labor were moved from farm to smoke house. Grandfather introduced me to the business of taking fish from barrels and laying them on the racks to cure. I liked this work fine, for a time, as it was fun to hear the talk of the men; they being full of salty wit and sharp sayings.

But I was beginning to feel the shortness of my tether so even the idea of school was welcome, making me look forward to it with pleasure for the first time in my life, thought I'll admit it was being off with the boys I craved rather than any hankering after knowledge.

On a bright Monday morning Ella and I started out, books under our arms and lunch pails swinging.

Everyone had been so good to me so far, I went all smiles and friendly up the school house yard. Then I received a considerable jolt to my confidence. As we drew alongside, a bunch of boys, my age, backed off, looking at me strange like. I heard someone mutter the word "Outlander."

Well, I had made my way into strange groups before, so I decided to lay low and take my bearing before I ran afoul and into a fight.

I was glad, though, when the bell rang and we all trooped inside. That was a school! There were seventy children in one room and a young lady teacher to handle them.

Every child had a different book, it being the custom to take whatever texts could be provided from home. Some studied geography and some reading. There was one little fellow who lugged a big dictionary and was studying it. I've always wondered if he ever got clear through to Z.

Ella and I were better provided for than most, because the Halls had fitted us out with regular readers, arithmetics, and spellers.

There were a lot of big fellows at the desks in the back who'd just come in with the fishing fleet. It didn't take us nor the teacher long to discover they were there just to pester and try her out, so there was noise and confusion, and interesting action to watch.

When recess came I kind of dragged myself out after the rest. The promise I'd given Ellen cramped me. I'd made friends before, wherever I was, even if it took a fight and a black eye to do it. So now, I was kind of lost as to how to proceed.

I wasn't lost long, though. A big fellow sauntered up, and saying the one word, "Outlander," he reached over, grabbed my cap, and threw it clear back under the school house, which was set on stilts.

I was boiling mad but I'd given Ellen my word, so keeping my hatch closed, I crawled underneath and got it, while all the children, even Ella, laughed fit to kill. I think it was her deserting me that hurt the worst.

At noon the same thing happened again and at afternoon recess and after school. I just couldn't figure it all out, and a wave of homesickness went over me until on the way to the farm, I crept behind a boulder to cry, big boy as I was.

The entire week was torment, though I determined not to let on at home. The word "Outlander" was a wall, worse than anything I'd ever faced. It was worse then being called "Shanty Irish" and "Swilly Pail."

Noons I sat alone to eat the lunch I could hardly swallow, for the lump in my throat, and nights I went to sleep dreading the coming day.

By Friday I was fair desperate, ready to throw the whole thing up and beg to be taken to the mainland or even the reformatory. Anything, to get away from the cap throwing and that taunt, "Outlander."

At recess Friday afternoon a big bully stepped up, starting to grab my cap, as usual. Before I knew what I was doing I'd shouted, "The first one that touches me will feel my fist," and out shot my arm, hitting him on the jaw and sending him flat.

I calculate it was an accidental providence that guided my blow rather than any great skill. I was standing on the rise above him and he was off guard, not expecting me to show any spunk or fight, else I'd never have landed such a broadside.

If this had been a bunch of Irish toughs my troubles would have been over and my place established, but such was not the case. The big fellows left me alone afterward, admiring my spunk, but the children gave me a wide berth until everywhere I went, amongst people, I'd think I would hear them muttering, "Outlander."

I was ashamed to let on about the business at home. The old folks were so good to me it seemed fair ungrateful to make complaint, but I determined to clear out soon as I could; the lonesomeness hemmed me in worse than any closed windows ever had.

Chapter 10
The Rescue

Providence stepped in and lent a hand in such fashion as to end the ostracizing I'd been subjected to. Behind my homesickness I'd developed a great ambition to live down the name of "Outlander" and to be called an Island boy.

My deliverance came in this fashion:

On Saturday afternoon Grandfather gave me leave to take the rest of the day off, to join the children where they were playing at the edge of the pasture woods. Hating to admit they'd have none of me, I went out anyway and hung about the boulders, longing to take part in their game of Indian and Scouts. As it got more absorbing I drew closer and closer until I was hiding behind the big pudding rock on which they'd built a fire.

While I sat watching, a little girl by the name of Clara Perry left the rest and came to the foot of the rock to play alone. A gust of wind blew some sparks from the fire, causing one to fall on her cotton dress, which burst into flames, like it was tinder. She screamed and ran toward me, so I was able to catch her and throw her down.

The cattle had made deep tracks in the muddy earth and these were filled with water from a recent rain.

"Fire! Fire! Help! Help!" I yelled at the top of my lungs, all the time rolling her and throwing on mud and water.

The children came on the run, but by the time they reached us the fire was out, though I was still yelling for help and Clara was crying at the top of her lungs.

She was a mess. Every stitch of her clothes were burned off except her woolen underwear, which had saved her life. She was covered with mud from her head to her heels. I'd sure done a good job of plastering her, and myself too.

She kept crying; saying her mother would whip her for sure for ruining her dress. We all discussed what was best to do and ended up by all trooping over to her grandmother's house, where the child was petted over and cared for.

Word spread around the Island fast that Mr. Hall's boy had saved Clara Perry's life, with his quick wittedness. Down at the store even the old tars praised me, until I forgot my troubles and felt pretty good.

Well, as I said in the beginning, Providence played her hand and that's how I became an Island boy. In their excitement over the fire the other boys had clean forgot I was an Outlander.

Chapter 11
Wandering Feet

After having been lonesome and hungry for boy company all summer, it seemed as though I couldn't get enough of being with a crowd and of games and fun.

I calculate I'd been good longer than was natural to me and in the ordinary way of things was about due to backslide. I paid no heed to Grandfather's warnings, and headed into trouble as if a three-reef gale was driving me into one scrape after another.

I'd good company, too—in the form of Will Ames and Alexander Perry. A person never realizes the joy of friends until he's been a time without any.

Will was full of wit and laughter, and quick and strong, while Alexander was more cautious, but every bit as full of boy courage. The three of us set sail on many a venture, such as only boys living by the sea can know.

I'd more work to do, at home, than either Alex or Will; so I was put to the constant temptation of skimping on my jobs, to be through in a hurry. I wonder that the old gentleman could have been so patient. He was firm and held me steady; for which I've always thanked him.

On Saturday after the fire, I was promised the afternoon if I'd get all my chores out of the way by midday; so I split wood and cleaned the barn, and filled the water buckets in a hurry—hardly waiting to bolt my dinner before I was off to Alex's house.

Will was there before me, and the three of us played "Annie over the cow shed" until we lost Alex's ball; which was made of twine covered over with the top of an old kid glove. After trying a rock, which was too heavy, Will said, "We need something soft."

The softest thing in sight was a setting hen near by; so up I grabbed her and yelling to Alex to catch, I sent her over—squawking and flapping. It was some stunt to catch her and the best sport we'd had yet. Ever once in a while we'd have to take time off to sit down and laugh.

The fun was just getting good when out came Mrs. Perry, madder than the hen.

"Here you boys, give me that hen quick! My soul and body! I've worked for three weeks to get her to set and now you've scared her so she'll leave her eggs for sure. You, Alex, go straight in the house until I can get in to tend to you. Stephen, you and Will make tracks for home and don't come back here until you get a little sense. I'll speak to your folks about this afternoon's business. Likely you'll get what's what, same as Alex."

I ran for home, hard as I could tear, and started carrying wood; though the box was nowhere near empty.

"Why all this sudden helpfulness?" asked Grandmother, looking suspicious. Making no explanation, I went right on working; and she let the matter drop.

Probably Mr. Perry quieted Alex's mother down, because the matter didn't reach Grandfather's ears until a long time after.

Having got by so well with the Perry affair, I felt considerably braver. School was getting tiresome and as I'd always run off when I pleased, I just stayed away the following Monday.

It wasn't hard to slip away from Ella. I'd meant to get Will and Alex to join me but I got sidetracked by running into Sam Piper, as he was leaving the house.

"Where's your ma today?" I asked.

She was a widow woman, left to fend for herself and Sam by working out.

"Oh," said Sam, "she's working the other side of the Island today. Why?"

"Let's play hooky," I coaxed, "and go lobstering down on the beach. Your Ma will never know the difference if we write our own excuses, and I'll bribe Ella not to tell."

This sounded good to him; so we hid our dinner buckets under the back stoop, and taking a pail with us, went to the beach.

There were plenty of little lobsters just waiting to be caught and we soon had all we could carry. We'd seen the folks put them in hot water so we built a fire in the kitchen stove, filled the tea kettle with lobsters, and left them over the blaze while we went out to play.

In the meantime, Mrs. Piper got through with her work early and started for home. As she went into her yard she thought it was funny so much smoke was going up the chimney, but decided there had been more coals in the range than she figured.

She hung up her shawl and set about to make tea. The kettle seemed heavy, so she poured some of the water out, and that was when she got suspicious. The water was red, and when she took the lid off, there were our lobsters.

She was waiting for us in the doorway, as we came up from the beach, and with scarcely a glance for me, she grabbed Sam by the ear and slammed the door. His howls filled the air—so I knew it was no place for me.

I couldn't go home and I dared not go to school; so I hung around the woods all afternoon, waiting to waylay Ella. It wasn't much fun being all alone and I began to kick myself for my foolishness.

It got so late, I decided I must have missed Ella and figured I'd best go home, take my medicine and get the whole thing over with. There wasn't much chance of her keeping still without pay.

I sneaked into the shed and cut my wood first thing. When I went inside nobody said a word about where I'd been; nor was it mentioned during supper, so I decided Ella had stood by me better than I'd expected.

After prayers the old Gentleman called me to him and I braced myself for a whipping, but he never laid a finger on me. He just said, "Stephen, I'm disappointed in you. It's about time for you to pull in your horns and settle down. Seems as though you need to ponder a little and get your bearings. Now, come Saturday, you go to the root cellar and sprout potatoes. While you're there you can think over the foolishness you have been into."

With a Saturday in the root cellar facing me, and Ella acting so virtuous, the work dragged terribly. Forgetting what Grandfather had said about thinking over my sins, I laid plans to outdo Ella's virtue by having me a good time while below.

I hid materials down there for a kite and got all set to enjoy myself. I fixed up a box to sit on while sprouting potatoes, or pretending to, and a box to hide the kite things in—in case Ella came spying about to gloat over me.

Saturday came and down I went and got myself all set for the day. I waited until I heard the women moving around upstairs, and then got my kite things out. I sprouted and whittled by turns. The thought of fooling Ella and the excitement of her frequent trips down buoyed me up.

After dinner it wasn't so much fun. Ella went off somewhere and I felt lonesome and shut in. The smell of dampness and spoiled potatoes seemed to fill the air; and I got all worked up and in a sort of frenzy. Somehow, in leaning over, I let the knife drive into my leg—cutting a deep gash. It bled considerably, so I was sure I would die. By using the kite string for a swab I got the blood stopped, but that did not stop my crying. I imagined how sorry they'd all be if they came down and found me lying dead, after being shut in the cellar. The make-believe was so real, it was a surprise to find myself alive.

I'd cut both my sock and underwear, so I changed my socks around. Sobered down by then, I sprouted more potatoes during the afternoon than during the morning.

When Grandmother discovered the cut in my underwear, next wash day, I had considerable explaining to do; but she never knew the knife was trimming kite sticks instead of potato sprouts.

You'd have thought a day in the cellar would have cured my wandering feet. I guess likely Grandfather figured the habit of running off was hard to cure, and required time and forbearance.

A few weeks later, instead of going straight home from school one afternoon I went to Philbrook's pasture with the boys, to play ball.

It was almost dark when Will called, "Look out, Steve! Here comes the old gentleman."

I started for home on the run. As I passed Grandfather he reached out and gave my ear a cuff.

"Stephen, I did not think this of you. Go home and get to your wood."

That is all he said, and it was the only time he ever laid a hand on me in punishment. It was enough, though, to make me realize there might be a limit to his patience.

Chapter 12
Life as an Islander

As winter came on the days grew shorter; a body had to hustle home from school if chores were to be done before it was pitch-dark. Even with hurrying we mostly finished the barn work by lantern light.

The fleet was safe in the harbor and all but a few boats were laid up, so the social life of the Island took up from where it had left off at the beginning of the fishing season.

All hands were thankful for the letup from the never ending drive of summer work. For a bit they could settle down to make the most of the breathing spell. By that, I don't mean they were idle; for the men had gear and nets to repair and the women had their house work.

There was time in early fall for chopping bees, and in the winter for singing schools and spelling contests. Best of all were the dances, with the fiddle scraping and all ages stepping it off. Then there were the socials at each other's houses, with kissing games and forfeits for entertainment, and refreshments that make my mouth water just to think about.

Having no shows to go to nor made to order fun, we worked up our own entertainment, and to my way of thinking we had a better time than young folks nowadays.

Will and Alex and I hung around Young's store every chance we got, listening to the talk of the men who gathered, this being a meeting place and sort of social club. They swapped yarns, each trying to outdo the other with tall stories, and argued the merits of the various fishing craft and kinds of gear. It was a liberal education for a boy, and while to an outsider they might have seemed a cranky and independent lot, I understood it was just their way of speaking.

During the war, in particular, the arguments waxed hot and heavy. Being the Island was half Democrat and half Republican, there were times that they almost came to blows during the evening sessions.

It was mostly foggy and cold, with sudden squalls that blew a gale you could lean upon; so houses needed to be caulked tight to keep the driving spray out. There were times the whole place would tremble and the roar of the ocean would fill the air.

Ella and I were free to ask our playmates in whenever we pleased; so the old house was filled with fun and laughter.

Our favorite times, though, were during the evenings. We'd gather around the stove or occasionally the fireplace, listening to Grandfather spin yarns.

We made a snug and comfortable picture, those evenings; Grandmother knitting, Grandfather in his great armchair and we children sitting about on the floor. Sometimes for a treat we'd roast apples or chestnuts. We didn't raise apples on the Island, so Grandfather had ours shipped in from the mainland and there were always a few barrels stored in the cellar.

On those long winter evenings he told us about the first Halls who settled the Island, and how that first Ebenezer was killed by the Indians, and his house burned down and his wife and family—all except the oldest boy who was at sea—taken captive, and how the wife escaped and made the journey from New York back to Falmouth on foot.

That was a game we played over and over, always letting Ella play the part of Ebenezer's wife.

Our favorite story was the one about the fight between Old Hall and Old Young, as to which should be King of the Island. It was decided that whomever could shout the loudest from the top of Mount Ararat should win. Well, Old Hall yelled and sat down, well satisfied. Old Young shouted so loud that Old Hall got up and, shaking his hand, conceded the victory.

That was a game we played on top of Mount Ararat. We always let Will be Old Young, being as he could yell the loudest.

There were stories about the British privateers, the pirate fleets, the shipwrecks and the War of 1812. There was no end to the tales about the bravery of the light house keepers. Then there were just yarns, some unbelievable so that Grandfather's eyes would snap and twinkle as he told them.

One night, after telling an extra whopper, he said, "Do you believe it?"

Little George Shultz piped up, "I'll be dammed if I do."

Grandfather never made a sound—just sat and shook all over. He was so tickled by the way George answered, he overlooked the profanity.

Sometimes, on a winter night, Grandmother made molasses candy in the black iron skillet. My, but it was good.

On Friday nights we fired up the old brick oven by filling it full of burning wood, so that in the morning, after raking the ashes out, Grandmother could put the jars of parboiled beans in to bake.

Being frugal, we baked the neighbor's beans, or they ours—turn about, so all the ovens didn't have to be fired up. We each had our names on our jars, and each were boiled and seasoned to suit the individual taste, then collected on a wheelbarrow and taken to the oven.

We were all neighborly folks, sharing each other's joys and sorrows, aiding one another in times of sickness or death, and lending a hand with heavy stints of work.

Pumpkin pie making was a yearly event we looked forward to. Mrs. Piper always helped and Amanda came down from upstairs, to lend a hand. Grandmother gave directions and all hands put in a day, with Ella running the errands to the cellar and I busy keeping the wood box filled.

We made the winter's supply of pies all at once, and then piled them on top of one another out in the winter pantry, where they froze so hard it took an axe to pry them apart.

They were fine eating until the beginning of spring, when they got soggy, after beginning to thaw.

On pumpkin pie making days the house was all fragrant with spices and Ella and I sampled until we were too full to eat our regular meals.

I tell you, the Island winters, in spite of cold and dampness, were wonderful to me.

The sharing of work and play, the bright warm kitchen and the sociability were something I'd never known before, and I'll always have a grateful memory of them.

Skating was a favorite pastime in the winter, with children and young folks making the ice sing with the sound of steel runners. There were two ice ponds on the Island, and clear, cold days you'd find us all out.

One such day I remember in particular. Our crowd had been playing privateer along the edge of the pond, with the privateers creeping through the alders to take the Islanders captive. This was our favorite game all fall, even creating several false alarms, just for the excitement, until our folks put a stop to that.

We tired of the game and went skating, each trying to outdo the other with fancy stunts.

All of a sudden there was an explosion like a ship's cannon being fired, and George Smith toppled out from the alder thicket onto the ice. Blood was running from his head and he lay there as if he were dead.

We were scared to death, being sure that privateers had landed and were headed our way. The big fellows grabbed George and we all went on the run for the nearest house, yelling that the privateers had come.

The alarm spread like wild fire and men came from every direction with such weapons as they could grab up.

In the meantime, the women at the house where we'd taken George set to work to revive him, after they discovered he was only stunned from a scalp wound and powder burns.

The men searched the shore lines and thicket but couldn't find any sign of a boat.

An injured boy and no sign of marauders looked mighty funny, so they went to the house to get our story and found George able to sit up and talk.

He owned up to the whole thing. He'd filled a toy gun with lead and powder and then set a match to it, thinking to give the skaters a good scare. It had back fired and it was a miracle his hand wasn't blown off.

We'd had enough of a scare from this event to cure us of wanting to make false alarms, and we turned our minds to other games than playing privateer.

Chapter 13
On the Water

During the winter most of the vessels were laid up because the harbor, not being properly sheltered, let the heavy winter gales blow in.

A few boats were kept at anchor to use in case of emergencies such as sickness or death; though often when these came the sea was so rough and heavy we were shut off from any chance of aid. Then, we cared for the sick ourselves. Grandfather was about as good as a regular doctor, so that many a soul owed his life to him. Some of the women were wonderfully handy with the use of herbs. Myself? I'd about as soon be dosed that way as with drug store concoctions.

On fair days the few boats in the water went out to fish, and of course I was wild to try my sea legs.

All fall I'd been begging to go but Grandfather kept putting me off, saying nobody wanted to be bothered with a boy who hadn't learned the knack of sailing.

I kept teasing Grandfather until he finally gave in and agreed that if anyone would have me, I might take a day off and try my skill.

I asked first one and then another, but they turned me down with excuses—saying I was too little or too likely to be a nuisance.

I was about to give up when I thought of Isaac Tolman, who I knew would do most anything to oblige Grandfather. He wasn't likely to refuse the Halls anything because of being beholden to Grandfather for a past favor. It was this way:

Years before, Isaac's brother Job had his arm shot off while duck hunting. He'd been out along the beach, and slipped on the icy rocks, causing his gun to go off accidentally. Well, Grandfather went every day for weeks, to dress Job's arm, and it was during the worst of the winter storms, too. What's more, not one cent would he take for pay. Tolmans had a bigger bump of gratitude than most, and went out of their way to do Grandfather a kindness whenever it was possible.

To get back to my story, when I asked Isaac to take me fishing he gave his consent and agreed to let me go, the first fair day. You can well believe it when I tell you that from then on I had my mind mostly on the weather, and spent my spare time getting pointers from Will and Alex on the art of fishing.

At last, on a day that was promising to be clear, word came that Isaac's boat would go out. I could hardly wait to get bundled up, grab my lunch and be off.

The vessel, a spanking fine hundred foot fishing craft, was ready to weigh anchor by the time I reached the wharf, and I'd barely scrambled aboard before we were off, the boat taking the swells like a bird. Wide and free she sailed, taking us out into Penobscot Bay.

I'm bound to say it was the most exciting day of all my life. I stayed up by the wheel pretending to myself that I was the skipper. The ocean rolled in long even swells and everything about the boat seemed to fairly sing, with the creaking of sheets and the whine of the boom against the mast. The crew, of which there were three, were on the lookout for fish and when a school was sighted the order came to heave to.

The fishing was done from along the side of the vessel, and to humor me, the men fixed me up with hooks, line and bait, same as the rest. I followed orders, baiting and letting out line, as they told me to.

We were fishing along easy, when all of a sudden I felt a powerful tug and something grabbed my line. It was too much for me to pull it in, so I yelled for help. The men, mistrusting what was on my line, stood by, ready with advice, but letting me do my own hauling in, so I could say I'd caught the fish by myself. I had lots of line, and they said:

"Let her go, Steve. Let her go. Let your reel out, and in, until you wear him down."

I did this, and finally, after what seemed like hours to my aching arms, I was able to haul in.

The men, standing ready with iron poles, grabbed it by the gills and with their help I pulled in my first halibut. It was about the biggest thing in the way of fish I'd seen.

The crew were about as excited as I was, and calculating that it would weigh about two hundred pounds, insisted that after it was sold, the money should be mine.

That evening my feet hardly touched earth as I hurried home. I burst into the shed, through the summer kitchen and into the kitchen shouting at the top of my voice, "I've caught a halibut that weighs two hundred pounds and Isaac says I can have the money from it!"

The folks were eating supper and the old Gentleman said, "Tut, tut, Stephen, you must not lie like that."

"Well, I did. Just ask Isaac and he'll tell you it's so. He's going to take it in to market tomorrow and give me all the money it brings."

After that, Grandfather believed my story. When I gave an account of the day's doings he acted mighty impressed by my adventure, listening as though I were grown up, and making me feel as if I were a real fisherman with a yarn to spin.

Fresh halibut were scarce in winter, so mine brought ten dollars, which Isaac said was a mighty good price.

I gave Grandfather the money as a gift, but I know now he had spent that and more for my winter clothes and school books.

I've caught many a fish in my lifetime, but none that ever gave me such thrill as my first halibut.

Chapter 14

The Drake

Days of bright sun and calm seas marked the approach of spring. Grandmother started worrying about my clothes, a matter which never bothered me much. I'd grown fast, thanks to good victuals and regular hours, so my arms were sticking out way beyond the ends of my sleeves. Everything I had was threadbare and patched until Grandmother said she was afraid my duds would not hold together through a school day. I'll admit I was powerful hard on clothes, what with playing and working and just plain carelessness.

During early spring Grandmother and Amanda had long discussions and Grandmother decided she would weave some material for a "Pea Coat" strong enough to last me a season.

When it was off the loom, she and Amanda cut and basted and fitted. It seemed to me I never got settled at my play, since I was always being called in for a fitting.

Grandmother had woven the selvage extra heavy and somehow made it run up the center of the back. There must have been something not quite right, because the bottom of the jacket at the center of the back curled up about two inches, like a little tail.

I had my misgiving s about the coat, but I hated to say anything after Grandmother had worked so hard on it, and I kept putting off wearing it on the pretense that I was saving it for good.

Finally Grandmother made me wear it to school. Will and Alex spied me first and admired the front view, but when they saw the rear view they burst out laughing and Will shouted, "Hey, fellows, look at the drake's tail. Look at Steve, the drake."

The name stuck and that's how it came about that I was nicknamed the Drake.

Chapter 15
Trouble from the Mainland

At the beginning of the war the Islanders were about half Republican and half Democrat, so it followed to reason that the Democrats sided with the Confederacy and the Republicans with the Union—thus making two factions that berated one another and just about ruined the neighborly ways we'd been accustomed to.

Grandfather was a staunch Republican and Union man; but he wasn't much of a hand to blow off and argue; so, boy-like, I didn't sense the trouble that was brewing. He refused to become involved in their fights or take sides with either crew of hot heads.

We boys went on about our own business of having a good time, with Democrat and Republican sons playing side by side in the militia we'd organized.

Thanks to the hours I'd spent around the Rockland sail lofts I knew the maneuvers better than the other boys, so that they made me captain. I drilled my men just as painstaking as though we really were going off to fight. I will say we made a pretty good appearance, what with two fixed up drums and a fife. Every boy stepped out proud and handsome. I'm telling you, we were a militia, as we marched up and down the wharf and across the pastures.

One evening as I was drilling my crew, a passel of giggling girls came down to the pasture to watch us. Contrary to my command, "Squad right!" the boys did squads left and marched into the girls. They held their formation and ran those girls on the double quick clean across the pasture. The girls set up a mighty cackling and pretence of being indignant.

Ella was one of the girls, and though I noticed she'd giggled plenty at the time, she let on to home that she felt mighty injured by the proceedings.

After she had let off steam, the old gentleman called me aside and said:

"A good regiment is always made up of gentlemen; if the captain is one, Stephen, the rest will follow."

I protested that I'd ordered squads right and Will and Alex had led them left. Grandfather fired right back:

"A real captain can make his orders hold and won't have mutineers on deck. Now, in the future you boys behave yourselves and act like gentlemen around the girls."

While we were drilling and maneuvering day after day the whole Island was driving straight into a squall, in the form of a second draft.

The first draft hadn't bothered much, as there were three Republicans to fill it, but when word of a second draft came out everybody knew secessionists would be called. The fire eaters howled and growled and the more they talked the more radical both sides got.

It was the beginning of the fishing season, so every able bodied man likely to be drafted, left with the fleet, which was putting out for Newfoundland.

When the draft servers came there were only two men left on the Island that weren't too young or too old, and one of those had a wry neck and the other a wooden leg.

The servers came again and again, but no one seemed to know where the fleet had gone or when they'd be back. Finally, the matter seemed to be dropped and we were left in peace.

In the fall the fleet came back to fish in our waters but they were cautious, keeping a sharp look out for strange craft and sleeping and eating aboard the vessels.

When nothing seemed to happen, they got braver still, and some of them slipped in a dory to spend the nights at home.

One evening, just at dusk, while our regiment were drilling on the wharf, we noticed a strange fishing dory come nosing in and we stopped our play to watch.

Three fishermen got out, and coming up to us asked where a certain fellow lived. They had their gear in the boat so we just supposed they were off some schooner, anchored out aways, and had come to visit friends or relatives.

Up steps I, being the captain, and asks could me and my men be of any service. They allowed we might, and asked if we would show them where this fellow lived. I disremember his name, but I do know that his younger brother was marching in the ranks. Since it was his house we were heading for it seemed no more than fair that he would lead the escort. So off we went, drums pounding and fifes playing.

When we got to the house the leader called his brother to the door, and the seaman handed him a paper, and turned to us, said how he'd admire to have us lead him to another party's home.

Not catching on to what was going on, we put another younger brother in the front and stepped off, high, wide and handsome.

We repeated this performance about three times before the alarm was out and from then on, no one was home.

Some of the boys were called in to bed and so we sort of deserted our fishermen and hurried home.

Next day the storm broke, mighty nigh disrupting the Island and causing bloodshed. We boys discovered our innocent look-ing fishermen were government draft servers and we'd helped them catch our own big brothers.

The poor peace maker always get the worst of a ruckus. Everyone turned on Grandfather, claiming he had notified the government of the fleet being in and had put me up to the escort-ing business.

Nothing either of us could say would change their minds, even the fact that two Republicans had gotten served.

There was talk of hanging and of burning our house down so we went to bed every night fearful that the hotheads would persuade the sober ones, and we'd either be burned out or Grandfather killed or maybe both.

Ella and I were kept in the house, and Grandfather lay at his moorings, not talking to anyone and keeping his own council.

Providentially, the fair weather held so that most of the troublemakers had to use up their energy in more profitable ways, and the work and salt water cooled them down.

Some of the secessionists were pretty offish to us for a time, but the rest were willing to let the matter drop.

Chapter 16
A Terrible Mistake

The same summer that the excitement over the draft was going on, I had an experience that sobered me down considerable and taught me more prudence than all the dressing down and whipping could have. I presume likely I was pretty brash and needing toning down, but it was too bad the lesson had to come at someone else's expense.

As I said before, the Philbrooks and Halls shared one barn together, that making it possible to have more loft space above and floor space below.

The barn swallows nested in the loft, and it was an interesting sight to see the young learning to fly. When the mothers pushed them of the nest, they would fall into the hay below.

Some of us boys conceived the idea of going aloft and catching them, though we had not figured what we would do with them after we caught them.

We had been warned over and over to stay out of the loft. Grandfather had explained the danger of falling through the holes where the hay was let down into the mangers below. In the first place, he didn't want us hurt, and in the second he calculated the cattle wouldn't relish hay our muddy boots had trampled down.

We paid no heed to him, and the first afternoon off from work we went up, forgetting all about George's little brother Isaac, who was tagging along astern.

We had great sport catching and penning the young swallows, and jumping from one pile of hay to another.

All at once we heard a dreadful cry and then a dull thud. We knew, without being told, just what had happened. Isaac must have gotten up somehow and fallen through a feed hole. We were scared to go down and look for fear of what we would find, but there was nothing else to do.

We found Isaac down below, lying as though dead, on a pile of straw at the edge of a manger. It was the hay sliding with him that broke the fall.

We gathered him up and carried him home to his mother. The scream she gave when she saw him was heart breaking. She took him in her arms and sent us hurrying for Mr. Philbrook, who was painting his boat, down on the beach.

I never, in all my life, hated so to take a message, and when I'd told him what had happened his face got white and he said in dreadful anger, "Didn't we tell you boys to keep off the hay? Now see what you've done. Stephen, go get your Grandfather."

Isaac lay unconscious for hours. It was pitiful, with him being no larger than a grasshopper.

Grandfather and the Philbrooks worked over him the rest of the day and friends and neighbors came in to lend a hand. Everybody was too busy and concerned to pay attention to us, so we sat miserable and fearful of the outcome, feeling if Isaac died we were little better than murderers.

In the evening Isaac came to, seeming not much the worse and no bones broken.

I was overjoyed, and rushing home, gathered up all my little treasures to carry back and lay beside him, on the bed.

Chapter 17

Spiritual and Physical Visitors

I remember more of my first year on the Island than of any other. I suppose it is because everything was new and exciting and the edge hadn't worn off from the joy of having a real home, and a man's guiding hand at the wheel.

My memory is hazy of the following years. Each one was pretty much like the other. The seasons brought their chores, regular as the tide: springtime the fleet went out and farm work started, autumn the fleet came in and off we went to school. Seems to me, looking back, there was a regular ebb and flow of life; so it is no wonder the Islanders were for the most part calm and steady.

Grandfather must have been powerful understanding of boy nature. He balanced work and play and talked things over with me, as man to man. When we got in too deep with our tricks and pranks I'd feel his steady hand at the helm, heading me into calmer waters; such times, though his face and voice were stern, there was always a twinkle in his eye.

Running the farm and salt house and laying down food for winter was a sort of family partnership, with the crew all lending a hand and sharing in the profits.

Grandmother's lameness got worse each year, so she depended on us more and more to do the running about.

One job we loved above all others was the gathering of the herbs.

Money was too scarce to send to the mainland for a doctor, except as a last resort, even if the weather permitted. There was a sort of herb lore passed down from mother to daughter, and Grandmother was a master hand at brews and poultices.

She'd gotten so that she couldn't gather herbs herself, and so she sent Ella and me after them. These gathering days were mighty pleasant. Sometimes Ella and I were given clearance papers to be gone all day, and starting out with lunch and baskets for herbs, we'd wander over pastures and through the woods, drinking in the warm sweet air until we felt all nice and clean inside.

There would be blue sky with clouds like balloon sails overhead, and the fields all covered with wild flowers; the beaches yellow like gold, and blue and gold mackerel shadows in the hollows of the waves. Sometimes we'd just lie on the hillside, chewing on a bit of spruce resin and let our souls stretch and grow.

Those days were like a purge that drove out all the meanness and let the sweetness of living flow in. Seems to me that is the thing town children miss the most.

When evening arrived we'd wander home with baskets filled with roots and grasses and in our hands great bunches of wild flowers. There was penny royal for tea, yarrow and nanny plum for a purge, sage and mint; sassafras bark, calomel and resin gum, and many other herbs I disremember now.

Back to home, there'd mayhap be clam fritters or blueberry tarts and Grandfather and Grandmother helping sort the herbs by lamp light, listening to our account of all we'd seen.

In the summer the wood house chamber was given over to the herbs and barks. We spread clean sheets on the floor and laid our barks and roots out to dry. We hung our herbs in little bunches from the rafters, so that the whole place smelled as though the woods and fields had trooped inside.

There were weddings and burying, the burying being too frequent, because of the consumption that got into men's lungs from too much cold and fog. And there were services without burial for those lost in watery graves, and only the markers in the burial lot to tell of their passing. It seems though we accepted birth and death the same as we accepted the weather. And, there were as many babies in the cradles as there were mounds in the graveyard. So, the Island held its own.

It always seemed to me the memories of the Matinicus dead stayed with us longer, as though our loved ones were about and we quoted their sayings and judgments for years.

That might account in part for a wave of spiritualism that swept the Island. Séances were held in darkened parlors and some claimed they received messages from their departed.

Grandfather did not hold with either the messages from the dead nor the mumbo jumbo some of them were saying over herbs, making charms against disease and shipwreck.

I never did know how it came about that Grandfather let them hold a séance in our house, being as he thought the whole business was plumb foolishness, at least that was the way he declared it to us at home.

I got wind of the meeting and passed the word to Will and Alex. We hid out in the yard until the lamps were turned low and then sneaked into the parlor unbeknownst to Grandfather.

When the chanting and mumbling started it was too much for us. Will let out a snicker and Alex and I started giggling fit to scare the spooks away.

Grandfather reached over and grabbing Will and me by the arm and nodding for Alex to follow, led us to the back stoop and set us down. I think he was kind of tickled too and glad for the excuse to get outside. But his face was grave enough as he said, "Now boys, I don't hold with all our friends' ideas, and I'll confess the séance business seems a mite ridiculous, but they are our guests and we're obligated to be courteous."

Warming up to his subject, he shook his finger at us and said, "Never, so long as you live, ridicule another man's belief. No matter how foolish it may seem to you, it's serious business to him and he merits your toleration and respect."

It was the living up to this teaching that made Grandfather loved by all and gave him the right to settle arguments and offer council.

One other lesson Grandfather and Grandmother taught us was the lesson of hospitality. Friends and strangers were welcome to share what we had. It was without question that visiting preachers would stay at our house.

Grandfather and Grandmother had never joined a church, there being none on the Island, but they prayed and read their

Bibles and listened while the visiting preachers held forth on their particular brand of salvation. We got a good many kinds, too, in the course of years.

I remember one radical preacher questioning the old folk's chances of getting to heaven, their never having taken what he called "The Step."

The parson go us so riled up that, boy though I was, and he my elder and a preacher, I shook my fist under his nose and shouted, "If the old folks aren't with St. Peter at the Pearly Gates to meet me when I die, why then I'll be having none of heaven, thank you!"

Chapter 18
No Man's Land

Long about the time a boy gets to be thirteen or so, he starts tugging at his moorings. Such was the same with us. After listening night after night to the yarns at Young's store the wind got in our heads so that we wanted to fill our sails and make off for foreign ports.

My old feeling of hating to be tied down came over me, and it seemed that the Island was getting smaller and smaller and closing in. The urge of pure adventure was pulling at Will, and Alex towed along to keep us company.

We were too old for pretending games and were aching to get our teeth into something we could actually taste, and this ache mighty near cost us our lives, in a way of speaking.

Down on the beach, at the cove, there was a dory that had been laid up for a year or two, as being beyond repair. This dory gave us our idea.

We included three other boys in our plans, after they had been sworn to secrecy, and laid out to go sea faring on our own. We worked for a good many weeks making the dory into a sailing vessel. We used a young spruce for a mast and sewed bits of canvas together for a sail. It wasn't hard to get pitch for caulking and oars and such. Every barn always has a mess of gear lying around. Food was hardest to come by, but we raided our folk's pantries and cellars for a little bit at a time, so that it wouldn't be missed.

We all worked hard at chores and in the fields and such, so the folks were willing to give us a day's holiday.

Finally, everything was ready and word was passed that we would set sail at sunup the following morning. I think we calculated on sailing down along the coast to Bath, although it is likely we were so intent on getting off that our plans for port were hazy.

At sunup the six of us were gathered on the beach, all ready with oil cloths and food. Will was captain, without question from any, although we argued every step of the launching and hoisting of the sail. It was run of the mill weather, so that the breeze was just moderate, but the minute it caught our sail over we were laid on our side. We all jumped up to reduce the sail before the boat turned over. To make matters worse the vessel leaked like a sieve and it took two boys bailing for dear life to keep her afloat.

We didn't give up easily, but we did calculate after considerable palavering that we had best make port at a nearby island the first night. With that decided, we set out with Will steering, two of us rowing, and two bailing like mad. It was hard work and the sun got hot toward noon, so that we were plumb thankful to draw alongside No Man's Land, drop anchor, and crawl out to stretch our cramped arms and legs. We were about starved and undertook to unload our grub, only to find it soaked and ruined.

Well, there was nothing to do but tighten our belts and eat wind pudding for dinner.

Alex calculated we might as well see the sights, seeing as we had come this far. So, off we went on a tour of investigation.

The island was uninhabited save for birds and such. It was covered with wild grasses, but not a thing a person could lay on to for food; none of us being hungry enough for raw sea fowl eggs.

We watched the sea pigeons and sand pipers and loons, while we stretched out on the warm sand to dry our clothing, but strange enough we didn't have much to say to one another.

After we had been there for about an hour Will allowed it was time to start home, and we all agreed. The prospect of rowing back in a leaky boat, and not one of us could swim, was kind of depressing and we were anxious to get it over with.

Going back, it was easier, as the boat had soaked up enough water to stop the leaking considerably, so we felt easier in our minds, even if the rowing was just as hard.

When the cove hove into sight we all heaved a big sigh and rowed for dear life, as though we'd been ship wrecked mariners afloat for days, instead of boys who had been less than a mile from home.

Chapter 19
The Price of a Soul

———————————

Henry Hall, who had immigrated to Illinois a few years before I went to the Island, was making his way by teaching school and farming. He kept writing letters telling of the wonders of the West. One thing in particular that impressed us all was his tale of plowing a whole day long and never turning up a stone. Some, who had never seen anything but New England farm land said that tale was a whopper, written just to match our fishing yarns.

Well, whether they believed about the stones or not, a lot of the men got all enthused; especially the young ones, until from the talk at Young's you would have expected in six month's time to find every soul had left the place.

All this was mighty unsettling to a young boy and of course I was wild to go.

I was seventeen years old, by now, and about ready for a man's place in the world, to my way of thinking. I'd been working out, earning a little as I went along, but mostly helping at home.

Everybody was mighty surprised when Grandfather allowed he might move to Illinois, if he could sell the place. He'd been pondering on it a long time and writing to Henry. He'd kept mum until his mind was made up. He allowed they would be happy to have me go along, but I'd have to get Ellen's consent in such a serious matter. I'd seen her about once a year and kept in touch through messages.

I went to Rockland and talked the matter over with her, but to my surprise she refused her consent, insisting she'd made other plans. Well, I begged and begged but she wouldn't give in. She'd arranged to place me as an apprentice to a stone mason there in Rockland, and was set on my settling down there. I balked at that—I could fairly feel the walls of the quarries shutting in on me. Me, who'd loved the open and dreamed of space and freedom. We argued back and forth for several days and finally make a bargain:

If I could get a berth on a fishing vessel I could go back to Matinicus; if not, I'd go to the quarries. I had to be satisfied with that.

Well, when I got back to the Island I discovered Grandfather had found a buyer for the farm and they were getting ready to leave.

He was disappointed that I couldn't go along, but when he found how rebellious I was about going to Rockland, he hustled round and found a berth for me on the Esperanza, Captain McFarland's boat.

Grandmother hurried and got my clothes ready and Grandfather made up what money I lacked to get me outfitted. Grandmother dropped everything to get my things all ready to pack: flannel shirt and warm wool sweaters; woolen socks and wristlets she'd knit. Grandfather had bought wool and cotton mitts, a suit of oils, and rubber boots and a sou'wester. They added bedding, all clean and warm, and pressed some money on me, so I'd be outfitted proper.

When Grandmother warned me about keeping my clothes in shape I might-nigh broke down and cried. I was so choked up I couldn't say a word when I kissed them goodbye, and the last I saw, they were standing with the tears running down their cheeks, too. None of us really ever expected to be together again.

Everything was a bustle down at the wharf with all hands hurrying to get the Esperanza loaded and ready for sailing. There is always a lot of last minute jobs and Captain McFarland was giving the orders so that all hands were stepping lively.

The Esperanza wasn't a fancy craft, like some of the high toned fishing yachts out of Gloucester; but she was sturdy and built to stand up under sail. She was deep and while she carried less canvas than some, I knew she would make up in dependability what she lacked in speed.

It was a nice sight to see the fleet getting ready, with topmast being sent up and sails dragged out and men shouting and laughing. There's something heartening about a fleet all ready for the season.

I reported to the Captain and then went to the fos'cle to store my gear.

It wasn't long before everything was ship shape and we were off for a season from Newfoundland to the Bay of Fundy.

Captain McFarland worked his crew and maintained strict discipline, but he was fair and no one had any complaint.

He furnished the boat, lines, and bait. In return each of us gave him half of our catch and sold the other half as our profit for the season.

We were levied an assessment to pay the cook and gave him over and above that a small percentage of our catch, so that he had a haul to show for the season's labor, too. If I recollect rightly, we each gave him ten dollars in cash, that season.

We slept and ate in the fos'cle, which was located well forward and was none too roomy. Along the walls were bunks for six and the rest was crowded with the stove and cook's gear. Fastened to the foremast, and hinged so that it could be raised between meals, was the table. It was like living in a triangle-shaped cave with the overhead swinging lantern casting shadows on the walls; and the air a mixture of the smell of oils and food and tobacco, all flavored up with fish.

Captain McFarland's cabin was to stern and joining it were bunks for the remainder of the crew.

The food was plain, but plentiful. Of course there was always fish in one form or another. If we were near harbor we had baker's bread, but out to sea we had to put up with fish biscuit, a sort of hard tack. Potatoes, salt pork, beans, pancakes and molasses completed our fare, with coffee to wash the whole down. We didn't know what it was to have fresh fruit or vegetables.

It was a hard life but one I soon got used to. Catching and dressing down, catching and dressing down. It went on day after day, providing there were any fish. In between were squalls to break the monotony and test our seamanship.

There were always some fun loving men aboard a schooner, who kept things jolly and amusing with their didos. And always, there was the singing. I guess that is where I got the habit of singing while at work.

I was seventeen but pretty much a green horn with a lot to learn. One of the crew was a boy younger than I, by the name of George. His father had died when he was small, so that he'd been raised upon his grandfather's boat, and was as able as any of the older men. It was irksome to me to be outdone by a younger boy, but try as I might, I could never equal him in skill.

One of the Islanders once told me that a seaman has to be born to it. He said, "Look at the seamen's babies in their cradles. They move their arms with an easy motion like rowing and when they coo it's like the tone of the sea in a shell. Yes sir, a man has to be born of sea faring folks to get the feel of it. It's in his blood and bone, and no matter how hard a landsman tries, he'll never make a good seaman."

I guessed perhaps he was right, I know I never got the hand of it the way Will or Alex did.

The first week out the fishing was fine, and everybody allowed we'd have a full hold and be back in port the first of all the fleet.

When Sunday came, I was sure put to it. I'd promised Grandfather to observe the Sabbath and a promise was a promise.

On the other hand, we had driven into a school of mackerel and it promised to be a good day for all hands. Debating inside myself, I finally followed the dictates of my conscience and went below to rest and read.

The crew made no objection, though they probably thought I was powerful foolish.

Even the cook was above, fishing along the side with the others, so it was uncommonly quiet and lonesome like in the fos'cle.

As I lay there a noise kept getting louder and louder in my ears. It was the flop of tails beating on the sides of the tubs, as the catch was drawn in, the sweetest sound of all to a fisherman's ears. It kept getting louder and louder, so that I knew we were in the midst to a whopping school, and the men were hauling in as fast as they could handle their lines.

"Thunderation!" says I to myself. "I can't stand this any longer," and up I went and took my place along the side.

And do you know, I hauled in three mackerel and that was the end of it. The school moved off and not another fish was caught that day.

That's how I sold my soul for three measly mackerel. The worst of it was I'd put a blight on the whole crew, so that the fishing was poor the rest of the season.

Chapter 20
Sailing South

Captain McFarland allowed the waters were too populous with fishing craft and the mackerel had all been scared away; so we moved into the Mount Desert neighborhood, as word had come that a school had been sighted there.

As we neared that locality the glass began falling and the Captain decided to make for harbor and gave orders everything loose on deck should be fastened down or stored below, and that I should get into the fos'cle and stay there. By the time we got the hatch battened down, the boat was plunging; in toward harbor the fog swept over us so thick you couldn't see a hand before your face. The shore line was rocky and dangerous and the Captain was unacquainted with these waters, so he decided to take a reef in the sail and beat it out again, into the blowing gale.

Down in the fos'cle I could feel the vessel heaving under me, and every time she dived the whole boat shivered and the wind sounded like a thousand devils screeching in the sails.

With the pitching and tearing I could hardly stay in my bunk, let alone sleep, so I decided I'd go on deck and see for myself what it was like. The waves were washing over the deck so that the skipper had lashed himself to the wheel and everything seemed afloat. I'd gone about one step when I ran into one of the men, his oils dripping brine. He yelled, "Who's there?"

Cupping my hand to my mouth I yelled back, "It's Steve. I've come up to help."

"Jumping Jehosophat!" says he, "You get below! We've got enough to worry about, without having to set someone to looking after you. Now, get!"

I went down, hating to miss the excitement and humiliated because George was allowed to stay above. Well, the whole night through we rode the storm and by morning both crew and boat were battered up considerable.

We fished up and down the coast making port to sell our catch and take on supplies. At such times the men hit the saloons first thing, so that it was not uncommon for the Captain and me to be the only sober men aboard. Sometimes he had a nip while in his cabin, but never enough to unsteady him.

I'd seen what drink does to the Irish and I vowed I'd never touch the stuff, nor tobacco either. Most folks think sailors are rough and drunken, but that's not true of all of them. There was many a teetotaler sailing those waters.

Such times as the crew were in the saloons or lying drunk, time hung heavy on my hands, so I was always glad when we put to sea again and all hands sobered up.

Chapter 21
The Race for Gloucester

———————————◼———————————

Captain McFarland claimed he had never seen a worse season, with storms tearing our rigging and a scarcity of fish. The whole crew was in the dumps so that there was precious little singing and joke making.

We had been from Newfoundland down to Cape Cod and had worked back up to the back side of Cape Anne when word came that the dories, out from Matinicus, were having better luck than the schooners. All hands agreed with the Captain that we might as well head for home and try our luck with the smaller craft.

As we sailed out around the back of the Cape we ran head on into a squall. It wasn't as bad as the one we'd rode in the Mount Desert neighborhood, but no one had any wish to go through any such as that again. The Captain decided to go around the Cape into Gloucester Bay and make for Gloucester Harbor, where we'd sell our catch.

The sky was dark and lowering with great banks of clouds rolled up, and the sea rolling so high it seemed like every wave would close over us. Captain McFarland ordered the hatches closed and a reef taken in the sails. There was a fearful wind blowing into the bay, but he knew those waters well, and the crew welcomed the chance to try their seamanship.

As we rounded the Cape, we saw one of the boats from the yacht fleet just ahead of us, making for the same port. She was one of their crack vessels with a reputation for speed.

The Esperanza wasn't any racing craft, but she had a lighter rigging than the yacht, which was in her favor in heavy seas.

All hands, even the cook, were on deck. When we sighted the yacht a half a mile away the word was passed that we'd give her a run for her money. The Captain began to shout orders and the crew to jump at his command. I never did see Captain McFarland so strung up as he was that day and the rest of us were half crazy, too.

We fairly flew before the gale, climbing and plunging until you'd have thought we would plough so deep we would never come up.

I was under the weather rail and hanging on for dear life, shouting myself hoarse above the whine of booms, the wind in the sheets, and the roaring of the sea.

Neck and neck we raced, both vessels showing as clever seamanship as I ever saw, and both entering the harbor at once, so that we allowed it was a tie.

The wind and waves had washed us clean of the doldrums, so that the fos'cle seemed more like it should that night, with laughing and singing and a deal of back slapping.

Next day we sold our catch and after taking on supplies, headed for Penobscot Bay and home.

I'd been dreading the return to the Island, as I knew it would never be the same with Grandfather and Grandmother gone. Word reached us, out of Gloucester, that the sale of the farm had fallen through, and the old folks had given up the idea of going to Illinois. This news heartened me up considerable and I could hardly wait to get home.

All hands were glad when we were anchored safe in Matinicus Harbor, calculating the whole voyage had been ill-fated from the first. As for me, I had an uneasy feeling that the sale of my soul for three measly mackerel had cast a spell on the luck of the all the crew.

Chapter 22
Six Hundred Fish

The Esperanza lay in harbor the rest of the season, the men going out in dories to fish, but sleeping and eating aboard her. Sundays I left the vessel and went home—mighty thankful for Grandmother's cooking, and the chance to be with Alex and Will again.

Grandmother had a conniption over the shape I'd let my clothes get in, and while she berated me, she scrubbed and mended until I was presentable. And then she scolded some more, because she said the minute she got me cleaned up, I was off to spend my time with a pretty girl. I will admit, I liked the girls and a few of them seemed to return the compliment.

It did seem as though we got shut of our bad luck by returning home. I wanted George to go into partnership with me in fixing up our own dory, but he would have none of me, so I was obligated to get a berth with Mr. Philbrook on one of his small boats.

Fishing was good, and though it was about the end of the season, I made up in part for the bad luck I'd been having. I remember one catch in particular:

Out in the bay we ran into the biggest school of mackerel we'd yet seen, and we were kept busy pulling in over the side of the dory, picking them off and baiting hooks again.

At the end of the day, when we counted them out, my share was six hundred fish. I was already tired, but my work had just begun, because they had to be cleaned and salted down before morning.

I got out my knives, fixed salt, carried water, set my table up and fell to work.

There were five things I had to do to every fish:

First, split 'em!

Second, gut 'em! That is, cut the entrails out.

Third, wash 'em!

Fourth, fat 'em! We ran a wooden handled tool, with a ball of lead on the end, along the side of the back bone, to make them look fatter. To my mind that was all humbug, as we sold them by the weight and not the looks.

Fifth, salt 'em!

Five things I did to every fish, before it was packed in the barrels and I can tell you, my arms were tired by the time I'd put six hundred fish down, two hundred to a barrel.

And, to top all of that job, I had to grind trolling bait for the next day's work.

I'd barely tumbled into my berth before Mr. Philbrook was shaking me awake, and yelling that the boats were about due to leave the harbor.

I'd dropped into my berth without undressing and by the time my head struck the bed, I was sunk forty fathoms deep in slumber. I stumbled on deck, so groggy with sleep I could hardly steer a course. Grabbing up a mug of coffee and a hunk of bread, I tumbled overboard into the dory.

I've done many a hard day's work in my lifetime, but of them all that stands out clearest in my memory.

Chapter 23
The Guy Mannsring Bucket

In late August storms and heavy fogs kept us laying idle in the harbor. One bad day word came to the Esperanza of a shipwreck off the southwest point of the Island. All hands crawled into oils and made off to aid in the rescue.

She was aground all right, with her hull stove in, but all the crew got off safe and there wasn't much to do, at least until the storm let up.

The vessel was the Guy Mannsring, bound from the States to Nova Scotia. When we learned she was English, we young fellows were all for letting the crew, who weren't in any danger, fend for themselves. We had no love for the British, having been brought up on tales of the Revolutionary Shaving Mills and depredations of the Privateers.

Grandfather, Mr. Ames and Captain McFarland shut us up and made us lend a hand. Mr. Ames took the Captain and mate into his house and we helped set tents up on the beach for the rest of the crew.

There always was a feud between American and British seamen—so it was not long before taunts and insults were passing hot and heavy. And, fists began flying between our rougher men and the shipwrecked crew. In spite of the older hands, considerable pillaging of the vessel went on under cover, though no one would admit to it. Before the trouble got too bad between us, a Nova Scotia boat picked up the stranded crew and a Boston salvage company bought what was left of the wreck.

The salvaging was mighty interesting to watch. Divers went down, during low tide, and ran chains under the vessel. These were fastened onto buoys and flat boats. At high tide the chains were raised and the wreck was brought up and swung around onto the beach. Most of the material in it was broken up and shipped away to Boston.

All the young fellows had lent a hand with both the rescue and the salvaging, so we figured it wasn't exactly stealing to take whatever happened to be handy. I know I calculated I had some pay coming to me in some way or another.

My hands fell on a bucket which looked mighty usable, but it was like a hot potato which I could neither hold nor drop.

First I hid it in the smoke house, but I was afraid Grandfather would run onto it. Then I took it down to the bell cellar and hid it behind a pile of barrels, and tried to forget it.

A while later, my bait bucket sprung a leak Of course, the first thing I thought of was the hidden bucket, which was a first class wooden one.

At first, the men had kept their stolen buckets hidden out in the boats, but after a time they got braver, and Guy Mannsring buckets appeared on every side.

I sneaked mine out and hid it under a canvas in the boat one day, while Charles Hall, my fishing partner, was off on an errand. When we got to sea I pulled it out and right off Charles said, "Steve, where'd you get that bucket?"

"Why, I found it in the bell cellar, but I ain't saying how it got there."

"Well," said Charlie, "as soon as the Old Gentleman finds out he'll be mighty put out and you know it. Just keep in mind it's your bucket and do the lugging of it. I'll not touch the thing."

After we'd made port that night, and I'd started up the wharf with the bucket in my hand, who should we run into but Grandfather.

We stopped dead in our tracks, knowing Grandfather would spot the thing first off and sure enough he said, "Charles, where'd you get that Guy Mannsring bucket?"

"Oh," said Charles offhand like, "Steve found it somewhere."

We didn't fool the Old Gentleman one mite and I cringed under the look he gave me, but all he said was, "I'd not have thought it of you, Stephen."

I gave the plague thing a toss that sent it clear out into the bay, and was relieved and plumb thankful when it floated from sight.

The season closed about this time and I went home to live, with seventy-five dollars in my pocket for the summer's work. After paying what I owed Grandfather and laying by a little, I sent the rest to Ellen.

Chapter 24

Casting Off

During the winter I lived at home mostly, and worked out by the day, picking up a bit of money now and then.

There was plenty going on, in the way of fun all right. Will and Alex and I were off skylarking every chance we got, and all three of us cut a considerable figure around the girls. Ice skating, singing schools, socials and dances made the winter fairly fly.

It seemed as though we had hardly gotten settled down before it was spring and time to get under way again.

I shipped with Ezekiel Ames during my second season out, but I can't recollect a thing about that voyage. I know it must have been a good one, because I had one hundred and sixty dollars to show when the season closed. At Grandfather's suggestion, I sent a hundred dollars to Ellen.

The voyage on the Esperanza, looking back now, was a big and exciting adventure from beginning to end. By the next year it was just the same old story, and powerfully tame. First place, there were not as many storms. And secondly, we didn't move about as much. It was catching and cleaning, catching and cleaning, day in and day out.

While I was working, my mind was traveling a thousand miles away, mostly out in Illinois where Henry Hall was, and during the evenings on the ship I'd perch astern and dream of covered wagons and Indians and breaking sod. At night the fos'cle seemed so close and narrow, I couldn't hardly stand being that cramped.

There was a fever in my blood that set me in a frenzy to be off into wide spaces, and made the boat a jail that kept getting smaller and smaller.

Grandfather calculated I'd not be much good to myself or to anybody else, the way I felt. He said he'd been watching me all year and his conclusion was no ways hasty.

He talked with Ellen himself, and laid the whole matter before her in such a way that she finally gave her consent to let me go West, providing that Henry Hall would agree to find a job for me.

Well, letters passed back and forth between Illinois and Matinicus, laying plans and charting my course.

Henry promised to give me a home and work until such time as I could get a steady job, and to be responsible for my behavior until I got my bearings and could navigate alone.

Grandfather arranged for me to make the journey with a nephew of his, who had been visiting in Rockland, and was ready to go back to Illinois.

Word came, in early February, that Mr. Norwood had to leave quicker than he'd expected and for me to be in Rockland by that evening. The weather was bad and most of the boats were laid up, so it looked for awhile as though I'd not be able to get a way to go.

Grandfather and I hunted about and he finally persuaded Otis Abbot to let his stepson, John Burgess, take me on his boat. Otis had married Clara Perry—her who I'd saved from burning years before, and Otis and John allowed that they owed me a favor.

When the time came to leave, I almost backed out. I couldn't have believed it would be so hard to say good-bye to Grandfather and Grandmother. I thought my heart would break when Otis weighed anchor, and I shouted a last good-bye to Will and Alex.

It was a strange feeling, to be torn between the pull to go and the pull to stay.

We barely made it to Rockland, what with a heavy sea and shortness of time, so I didn't have much chance to ponder, until I was on board the train with Mr. Norwood.

It was my first train ride. The new sights and sounds eased the heavy feeling in my heart and before many hours my sails were set and I was ready for the voyage. The port my mind's eye saw was rolling fields, green like the ocean on a fair day, but solid under foot so that a man might travel to his heart's content without walls or water to hem him in.

Afterword

Stephen Cronin, born September 10, 1850, never saw his mother or brother again after leaving Maine. John, his brother, became a stone cutter, married and moved to Saint Cloud, Minnesota, where he and his wife raised three children.

Freeman Hall, whom Stephen called Grandfather, continued living on Matinicus Island with his wife until their deaths.

Stephen's trip west with the Hall's son Henry Edwin Hall took him to Roseville, Warren County, Illinois, where he lived with Henry and his wife Pamela. Stephen married Flora Chorley on April 14, 1879 at the age of twenty-eight.

When Henry and Pamela returned to Maine to combat Henry's tuberculosis in 1880, Stephen and Flora traveled to Kansas in a covered wagon, driving cattle and homesteading south of Patridge, Reno County. Together they raised five children.

Books About Matinicus Island

Islands Down East: a visitor's guide, by Charlotte Fardelman; Down East Books; 1984; ISBN 0892721898

Islands in Time: a natural and human history of the islands of Maine, by Philip W. Conkling; Down East Books; 1981; ISBN 0892724781

Matinicus Isle, its story and its people, by Charles Albert Eugene Long; Lewiston Journal Printshop; 1926; OCLC 16945281

Portrait of Maine, by Berenice Abbott and Chenoweth Hall; Macmilan Press; 1968; OCLC 448711

Tales of Matinicus Island: History, Lore and Legend; by Donna K. Rogers; Offshore Publications; 1990; OCLC 22753128

The Coast of Maine: a complete guide, by Nancy English; Berkshire House Publishers; 2002; ISBN 1581570589

The Coast of Maine; an informal history and guide, by Louise Dickinson Rich; Down East Books; 1975; ISBN 2723424

The Maine Islands in Story and Legend, by Dorothy Simpson;
    Maine Writers Research Club; Blackberry Books; 1987;
    OCLC 16705678

The Salt Book: lobstering, sea moss pudding, stone walls, rum
    running, maple syrup, snowshoes, and other Yankee doings,
    by Pamela Wood; Anchor Press; 1977; OCLC 2818703

Index

978-0-595-39149-3
0-595-39149-4

Printed in the United States
95305LV00005B/67-69/A

9 780595 391493